The Myth of Gender Equality

By Drake Shelton

Louisville, Ky
3/18/2015

Deut. 28: 58 "If you are not careful to observe all the words of this law which are written in this book, to fear this honored and awesome name, the Lord your God, 59 then the Lord will bring extraordinary plagues on you and your descendants, even severe and lasting plagues, and miserable and chronic sicknesses. 60 He will bring back on you all the diseases of Egypt of which you were afraid, and they will cling to you. 61 Also every sickness and every plague which, not written in the book of this law, the Lord will bring on you until you are destroyed. 62 **Then you shall be left few in number**, *whereas you were as numerous as the stars of heaven,* **because you did not obey Yahowah your God**.

Moses

"If human experience has established anything at all, it is the truth of that principle announced by the Hebrew prophet when he declared that the great aim of God in ordaining a permanent marriage tie between one man and one woman was 'that He might seek a godly seed.' God's ordinance, the only effective human ordinance for checking and curbing the first tendencies to evil, is domestic , parental government. When the family shall no longer have a head, and the great foundation for the subordination of children in mother's example is gone; when the mother shall have found another sphere than her home for her energies; when she shall have exchanged the sweet charities of domestic love and sympathy for the fierce passions of the hustlings; when families shall be disrupted at the caprice of either party, and the children scattered as foundlings from their hearthstone,- it requires no wisdom to see *that a race of sons will be reared nearer akin to devils than to men*. In the hands of such a bastard progeny, without discipline, without homes, without a God, the last remains of social order will speedily perish, and society will be overwhelmed in savage anarchy. "

R.L. Dabney, The Southern Magazine, January, 1871 Vol. 8, pg. 332

"Must not God be avenged on such a nation as this? His vengeance will be to give them the fruit of their own hands, and let them be filled with their own devices. He will set apart this fair land by a sort of dread consecration to the purpose of giving a lesson concerning this godless philosophy, so impressive as to instruct and warn all future generations. As the dull and pestilential waves of the Dead Sea have been to every subsequent age the memento of the sin of Sodom, so the dreary tides of anarchy and barbarism which will overwhelm the boastful devices of infidel democracy will be the caution of all future legislators. And thus, 'Women's Rights' will assist America 'to fulfill her great mission,' that of being the 'scarecrow' of the nations. "

R.L. Dabney, Ibid, 334

Introduction

What modern woman has the mental strength and honesty to acknowledge that all her problems are the creation of her own mind; her own Frankenstein monster?

In keeping with their Counter-Reformation, the Jesuit Order of the Roman Catholic Church has used the Epicurean Philosophy that they resurrected from the graves of Greece through their master disciple Descartes, to disenfranchise the common, moral, religious white man and has empowered the selfish, wicked white man, "nearer akin to devils" predicted by Dabney above. Before I begin I want to address those women who believe the Bible, and live to serve their husbands and further their race through a stable family. If that is you, the vitriol and anger that you will read in this essay is not directed at you. Peace to you and your family.

Before I display the bible's teaching concerning gender relations I want to sweep away all the presumptions of the western liberated woman.

There is no doubt that Christianity created an unnatural view of sex extending from their Gnostic theology with the early Fathers, and the rise of the asceticism and monasticism of Christianity in general. This is clearly stated in Kinsey's *Female Volume*, page 89. I exposed the Christian Monastic conspiracy in my recent book *Conquering the Verbal Sorcery of Christianity*.

The Jesuits have deceived our people to espouse the Enlightenment Philosophy and as was shown above, this has made Yah himself our enemy. Our race is being driven into Miscegenation and the women who refuse to bear any children are growing as well. Truly, we are being made a people few in number.

Feminist, Jody Day of Gateway Women states,

> "I truly believe that being a childless/childfree women is one of the unfinished businesses of Feminism and it is up to pioneers like us to say the unsayable, think the unthinkable and live our gloriously unacceptable (to others) lives so that this taboo can be busted right open!"[1]

Gretchen Livingston and D'Vera Cohn of the Pew Research Center state in their article *Childlessness Up Among All Women; Down Among Women with Advanced Degrees*,

> "The most educated women still are among the most likely never to have had a child. But in a notable exception to the overall rising trend, in 2008, 24% of women ages 40-44 with a master's, doctoral or professional degree had not had children, a decline from 31% in 1994.

---

[1] http://www.dreamcorner.co.uk/being-childfree/

By race and ethnic group, *white women are most likely not to have borne a child.*"[2]

Feminism is simply the development of the Enlightenment and the first and second French Revolutions. As we have seen for some time now, this was all a creation of the Jesuits. The Enlightenment was meant to destroy the Protestant Reformation while the French Revolution was meant to take revenge on the Catholic nations that suppressed the Jesuits in 1773, *Dominus Ac Redemptor Noster.* The Enlightenment begins with Jesuit trained Galileo and his Heliocentrism, followed by Jesuit trained Descartes and his revival of "ancient Greek opinions concerning atoms".[3] The women's right's movement was begun in 1791 with the French playwright and political activist Olympe de Gouges. She published the Declaration of the Rights of Woman and the Female Citizen 1791, which was modeled on the Declaration of the Rights of Man and of the Citizen of 1789. Gouges argued for universal equality of the sexes. Later in 1848, these principles would be enshrined in The Declaration of Sentiments by Elizabeth Cady Stanton and Lucretia Mott. I have refuted the Enlightenment in my recent book on the South and will continue to do so in a future book on Atheism. Dabney refuted the Enlightenment view of human rights in his *Discussions* Vol. 3 Philosophical, "Anti-Biblical Theories of Rights".

---

[2] http://www.pewsocialtrends.org/2010/06/25/childlessness-up-among-all-women-down-among-women-with-advanced-degrees/
[3] John Robertson, *The Case for the Enlightenment* (Cambridge University Press: New York, 2005), 96

Fast Facts About Male Exploitation In The United States

1. Only men are required to be drafted and sent to die for the United States. The Selective Service System of the United States Government states,

> "Almost all male U.S. citizens, and male immigrants living in the U.S., who are 18 through 25, are required to register with Selective Service."[4]

2. Taking paid work and household duties into consideration, Fathers worked 47 hours a week, while Mothers worked 39 in 2011.[5]

3. Men are the slaves of women.

a. They do the hardest and most dangerous jobs to keep women's lives comfortable. The U.S. Bureau of Labor Statistics, *Census of Fatal Occupational Injuries Charts, 1992-2012* page 8 shows that 92% of occupational fatalities were men.[6]

Page 19 shows that the most dangerous jobs are:[7]

1. Logging workers
2. Fishers and related fishing workers
3. Aircraft pilot and flight engineers

---

[4] http://www.sss.gov/fswho.htm
[5] http://www.usatoday.com/story/news/nation/2013/03/14/men-women-work-time/1983271/
[6] http://www.bls.gov/iif/oshwc/cfoi/cfch0011.pdf
[7] http://www.forbes.com/sites/jacquelynsmith/2013/08/22/americas-10-deadliest-jobs-2/

4. Roofers
5. Structural iron and steel workers
6. Refuse and recyclable material collectors
7. Electrical power-line installers and repairers
8. Drivers/sales workers and truck drivers
9. Farmers, ranchers, and other agricultural managers
10. Construction laborers

Consider also garbage men, taxi drivers, firefighters, miners, and police officers. According to the U.S. Department of Justice, Bureau of Justice Statistics, 85% of all police officers are men.[8]

According to the United State's Department of Labor's *20 Leading Occupations of Employed Women*, we see that the jobs women do are considerably safer and less stressful jobs than men perform.[9]

b. Outnumbered over two to one, 258,000 Southern men died to defend Southern women from the invasion of a Northern Army.[10] The same story runs today as well. *2011 Demographics Profile Of The Military Community,* Updated November 2012, page 17 shows that 85.5% of active duty military personnel are male. Yet this does not imply that the 14.5% female population is involved in combat.[11]

---

[8] http://www.bjs.gov/content/pub/pdf/wle8708.pdf
[9] http://www.dol.gov/wb/factsheets/20lead2009.htm
[10] http://www.civilwar.org/education/pdfs/civil-war-curriculum-stats.pdf
[11]http://www.militaryonesource.mil/12038/MOS/Reports/2011_Demographics_Report.pdf

In fact, *The Washington Post* states in its article, "Three women pass Marine 'grunt' test, but Corps holds off on letting them in infantry" by Craig Whitlock, November 20, 2013,

> "For the first time, three enlisted women have passed the Marine Corps' grueling infantry course, carrying the same rifles and lugging the same 85-pound packs on the same 12-mile hikes through the piney woods of North Carolina as the men. The female Marines are scheduled to graduate Thursday at Camp Geiger, N.C. — a historic development as the U.S. military prepares to open ground combat forces to women."[12]

It appears then that the G.I. Jane persona that we have been led to believe has regularly existed for so long, is actually a myth.

Clearly then, women get paid less, not because they are women but because the men are taking the most risk and subjecting themselves to the most danger. Also "Men Earn More Money and Promotions Because They Work More Hours Than Women".[13]

c. Women complain about the glass ceiling that keeps them from ascending into the highest positions

---

[12] http://www.washingtonpost.com/world/national-security/three-women-pass-marine-grunt-test-but-corps-holds-off-on-letting-them-in-infantry/2013/11/20/6e04f164-51f6-11e3-9fe0-fd2ca728e67c_story.html

[13] http://www.huffingtonpost.com/rebecca-shambaugh/talent-development-women_b_3640094.html

of power in America, yet more men are trapped in the "glass cellar" that keeps men in jobs with the most danger.

d. Men are expected to be the unpaid bodyguards of women. They are to receive violence but never return it. They are expected to give up their seats for women and at one time they were expected to stand up as a woman entered the room and were also expected to bow to them. They also help women put on their jackets. Men are often seen walking along side of the highway in desperation. Who ever saw a woman in this condition? Men are also more likely to be homeless.[14]

e. Men are less likely to be able to go to college.

> "On a national scale, public universities had the most even division between male and female students, with a male-female ratio of 43.6–56.4. While that difference is substantial, it still is smaller than private not-for-profit institutions (42.5-57.5) or all private schools (40.7-59.3). The nearly 40-60 ratio of private schools was most surprising, though perhaps this is partly due to the fact that most all-female schools are private. Nevertheless, the female domination of higher education prevails across all types of schools."[15]

---

[14] http://www.nationalhomeless.org/factsheets/who.html
[15] http://www.forbes.com/sites/ccap/2012/02/16/the-male-female-ratio-in-college/

f. Violence against women is abhorred but violence against men is entertainment. We are the gladiators for women's amusement in Football, MMA, Boxing, Wrestling, Ice Hockey, Rodeos, Auto Racing etc.

Fast Facts About Female Supremacy In The United States.

1. The Government plays the bodyguard role for women in America.

a. "Across a wide range of jurisdictions the estimates are that mothers receive primary custody 68-88% of the time, fathers receive primary custody 8-14%, and equal residential custody is awarded in only 2-6% of the cases."[16]

This leaves the burden of two households on the Father. Is it then any wonder that "Divorced men are more likely to have heart disease, high blood pressure and strokes than married ones - are also 39% more likely to commit suicide"?[17]

Men are so ridiculed by other men for depression as if it was a sign of weakness, that when faced with suicidal thoughts, instead of seeking help men just commit suicide.

When I was in college I ministered at a detention center in Greenwood, Sc. Most of the men that

---

[16] http://www.huffingtonpost.com/robert-hughes/are-custody-decisions-bia_b_870709.html
[17] http://www.dailymail.co.uk/health/article-2440005/Divorce-mans-health-Separation-increases-risk-death-substance-abuse-suicide-depression.html

attended my Bible study were men in prison for failure to pay child support. And get this; if a woman tells you she is using birth control and isn't, if you get her pregnant she can still sue you for child support!

b. The fact that the men don't pay shows that women are not qualified to chose their lovers.

2. Breast cancer receives much more research funding and publicity than prostate cancer despite similar number of victims.[18]

3. Men commit suicide over 3 times the rate women do.[19]

4. "Across the industrialized world, women still live 5 to 10 years longer than men. Among people over 100 years old, 85% are women".[20]

5. "Males were nearly 4 times more likely than females to be murdered in 2008".[21]

6. Women spend the most money in America:

---

[18] http://www.cancer.gov/cancertopics/factsheet/NCI/research-funding
http://dailycaller.com/2010/10/05/breast-cancer-receives-much-more-research-funding-publicity-than-prostate-cancer-despite-similar-number-of-victims/#ixzz2sQwoRjD6
http://well.blogs.nytimes.com/2008/03/06/cancer-funding-does-it-add-up/?_php=true&_type=blogs&_r=0
[19]http://www.cdc.gov/violenceprevention/suicide/statistics/rates04.html\
[20]http://content.time.com/time/health/article/0,8599,1827162,00.html
[21] http://www.bjs.gov/content/pub/pdf/htus8008.pdf

"Female shopping trips are most important to the mass merchandiser and dollar store channels, while male shopping trips are of greater relative importance within convenience/gas, grocery and warehouse club outlets. Women spend more money per trip than men in all of the channels examined, but in many channels, the differences between the sexes are not as great as one might expect. Nevertheless, spending differences do indicate that women drive the larger stock-up or planned trips as they outspend males by $14.31 per trip in supercenters and by $10.32 per trip in grocery stores."[22]

7. It has been my life experience that women are far more competitive with each other than men are with men and when given power have shown themselves just as bloodthirsty if not more bloodthirsty and warlike than men. My fathers come from England. One of the reasons my Fathers left England was religious persecution. One of the most famous persecutors was Bloody Mary. She killed hundreds of Protestants by burning them alive for their religious beliefs. Queen Isabella engaged in War with Portugal and enabled the conquest of North America via Christopher Columbus. In recent years Margaret Thatcher, the "Iron Lady" engaged in the Falklands War.

---

[22] http://www.nielsen.com/us/en/newswire/2013/u-s--women-control-the-purse-strings.html

Feminism Hurts Women

1. Too many short broken relationships leaves modern women mentally and emotionally scarred. This serves to create huge masses of both men and women who seek revenge on the opposite sex at every opportunity.

2. The only way to enjoy this type of life is to harden yourself to the point where you become ruthless.

3. Your young years are the best to start having children and your best time to find a life partner. When you are out of college and in the work force you are not going to have the time or the opportunity to be around men you have known for years and can trust with your life.

4. Feminism makes men apathetic toward family roles and life in general. Man has lost his sense of leadership, masculinity and also his chivalry and it's all the fault of Feminist women. Not only do Feminists not believe that the woman was made for the man (1 Cor. 11:9), they view men as the great burden on humanity, full of sexual perversions and grotesque dependencies- a real life slobbering werewolf. He is to wear a dunce hat for all his life, and bear the guilt of all the sins in the world, especially if he is white. Moreover, the vast majority of Feminists have sex before marriage with multiple partners. Feminists want to have sex with as many men as they want and then when they want to get married to a good guy, he is just supposed to overlook all the men that have had their way with his wife to be and the mother of his children. Moreover, Feminism takes away his authority and makes the

word "Father" empty of meaning. Also, women are given preferential treatment in the divorce courts.

> "RESULTS For the entire sample, higher risks of suicide were found in divorced than in married persons. Divorced and separated persons were over twice as likely to commit suicide as married persons (RR=2.08, 95% confidence intervals (95% CI) 1.58, 2.72). Being single or widowed had no significant effect on suicide risk. When data were stratified by sex, it was observed that the risk of suicide among divorced men was over twice that of married men (RR=2.38, CI 1.77, 3.20). Among women, however, there were no statistically significant differentials in the risk of suicide by marital status categories.
> CONCLUSIONS Marital status, especially divorce, has strong net effect on mortality from suicide, but only among men."[23]

As a matter of fact a woman can divorce a man and take half of the family assets for no fault or wrongdoing on his part at all.[24]

The modern sports, drug and porn culture is a result of men seeing no incentive in committing to responsible family life. This leaves these "liberated"

---

[23] http://jech.bmj.com/content/54/4/254.abstract
[24]http://family-law.lawyers.com/divorce/do-i-need-a-reason-to-get-divorced.html

women mostly single as they ascend into their later years, bitter, and alone.

5. The Feminist attitude is unnaturally crass and pugnacious as a way to impersonate male toughness as an attempt to make men see them as equals. This makes men hate women and paints a proverbial target on the forehead of such women. It also creates chaos in the workplace.

6. The Feminist sexual revolution, pace Margret Sanger, has turned women into empty shells whose lives are primarily focused on appealing to the sexual desires of men.

7. The children of Feminists have no one to raise them but the media and the government public schools. This is creating a savage generation of children that cause their parents great grief.[25]

8. The Feminist sexual revolution has literally killed millions of girls in abortion clinics.

9. The Feminist sexual revolution has seen to the creation of an international human trafficking market where women are kidnapped and forced into sex slavery.

10. The Feminist sexual revolution has created a plague of sexually transmitted diseases.

11. Feminism sparked the Civil War, pace Harriet Beecher Stowe. This civil war created a more

---

[25] *Guilty: Liberal "Victims" and Their Assault on America* by Ann Coulter, 36-38

centralized federal government that created the modern monetary and tax system which steals so much money from Americans that women must work in order for a common family to survive.

12. Feminism has deceived young girls into thinking that they can govern their own lives. The problem is, young women are too controlled by their emotions to make well thought through decisions.

Example #1. Young girls follow their emotions and typically look for the bad boy. From what I have heard, young women, in their narcissism, think they can bring worship to themselves if they can change said bad boy. This experiment has resulted in a plague of tens of millions of aborted children and a population of mostly abandoned unwed mothers in America. According to the CDC's National Vital Statistics Reports (October 3, 2012), see tables 1 and 7, 40% of births in the US are to unwed mothers! Here we see that Feminism enfranchises the bad boy. And women wonder why there are no good men.

Example #2. When I was in college I was good friends with a young Latino girl. She was in love with my best friend. The year before our first year in college, he had offered himself to her at the time that she was in love with him. I asked her why she turned him down. She said, "I was too scared. I was overcome with emotion." A couple years later she had despaired of finding a good guy and married a savage police officer she knew little about. He turned out to be a violent man with a porn addiction. After having a child with him, she divorced him for multiple grievances. After this divorce she gave up on romance completely. Feminism is a disease.

White Men In Protestant Countries Have Made
All Of The Most Significant Accomplishments
Even After The Liberation And Higher Education
Of Women

In the Fourth Session of the Roman Catholic Council of Trent we Read,

"DECREE CONCERNING THE EDITION, AND THE USE, OF THE SACRED BOOKS

Moreover, the same sacred and holy Synod,--considering that no small utility may accrue to the Church of God, if it be made known which out of all the Latin editions, now in circulation, of the sacred books, is to be held as authentic,--ordains and declares, that the said old and vulgate edition, which, by the lengthened usage of so many years, has been approved of in the Church, be, in public lectures, disputations, sermons and expositions, held as authentic; and that no one is to dare, or presume to reject it under any pretext whatever.

Furthermore, in order to restrain petulant spirits, It decrees, that no one, relying on his own skill, shall,-- in matters of faith, and of morals pertaining to the edification of Christian doctrine, --wresting the sacred Scripture to his own senses, presume to interpret the said sacred Scripture contrary to that sense which holy mother Church,--whose it is to judge of the true sense and interpretation of the holy Scriptures,--hath held and doth hold; [Page 20] or even contrary to the unanimous consent of the Fathers; even though such interpretations were never (intended) to be at any time published. Contraveners shall be made known by their Ordinaries, and be punished with the penalties by law established.

And wishing, as is just, to impose a restraint, in this matter, also on printers, who now without restraint,--thinking, that is, that whatsoever they please is allowed them,--print, *without the license of ecclesiastical superiors, the said books of sacred Scripture*, and the notes and comments upon them of all persons indifferently, with the press ofttimes unnamed, often even fictitious, and what is more grievous still, without the author's name; and also keep for indiscriminate sale books of this kind printed elsewhere; (this Synod) ordains and decrees, that, henceforth, the sacred Scripture, and especially the said old and vulgate edition, be printed in the most correct manner possible; and that it shall not be lawful for any one to print, or cause to be printed, any books whatever, on sacred matters, without the name of the author; nor to sell them in future, or even to keep them, unless they shall have been first examined, and approved of, by the Ordinary; under pain of the anathema and fine imposed in a canon of the last Council of Lateran: and, if they be Regulars, besides this examination and approval, they shall be bound to obtain a license also from their own superiors, who shall have examined the books according to the form of their own statutes. As to those who lend, or circulate them in manuscript, without their having been first examined, and approved of, they shall be subjected to the same penalties as printers: and they who shall have them in their possession or shall read them, shall, unless they discover the authors, be themselves regarded as the authors. And the said approbation of books of this kind shall be given in writing; and for this end it shall appear authentically at the beginning of the book, whether the book be written, or printed; and all this, that is, both the approbation and the examination, shall be done gratis, that so what ought to be approved, may be approved, and what ought to be condemned, may be condemned."[26]

Here we see that it was the Protestant demand for Bibles that opened the Freedom of the Press in Protestant Nations. Subsequently, the Treaty of Westphalia which ended the failed Catholic War of Protestant Annihilation, The Thirty Years War, is, in defiance of the local University's denial of facts, the true end of Catholic dominance in Europe and thus the true end of the Middle Ages, introducing the modern period.

At this point the Protestant Nations explode with Scholarship, Culture, Literature, Art, and Science, created the highest Civilizations that have ever existed and have dominated the world since. The reason why this was possible is because the Protestant Reformation opened the press, which gave the Bible to the people and thus raised the people's morals and the Protestant Governments allowed freedom of thought and invention.

England had already entered their Protestant Golden Age with blessed Elizabeth, which produced Sir William Shakespeare but picking right up from Westphalia is the production of one of the greatest minds to ever exist, Sir Isaac Newton. Protestant Germany produced the great Lutheran Johann Sebastian Bach. The Protestant Dutch enter their Golden Age with Rembrandt (His Father was Dutch Reformed). The Protestant Presbyterian Scottish produced Adam Smith who invented modern

---

[26] http://history.hanover.edu/texts/trent/ct04.html

Economics and James Watt who invented the Steam Engine.

In grievous pain the modern Feminist will look upon this horrifying period of History and complain that there are no women participating in all of this glory because they were being systemically suppressed by the evil white man. In reply, I would simply ask the reader to consider the technological accomplishments that have taken place since women began to receive Professional Education in the mid 19th Century.

The following is taken from *Technology A World History* by Daniel Headrick published by Oxford University Press, 2009 where we see a list of the most significant inventions since the mid 19th century. The text says on page 138,

> "Almost all technologies introduced since World War II originated in the United States, Germany, Great Britain or the Soviet Union."

1. Beginning in the 1860s, William Kelly of Kentucky as well as Henry Bessemer (Englishman) and Sidney Gilchrist Thomas (Englishman) invented the methods used to produce enough Steel to enable industrial Mass production.[27]

2. Italian Alessandro Volta invented the battery.[28]

---

[27] 112-113
[28] 113-114

3. German Ernst Werner Siemens and the Belgian Zenobe Gramme invented dynamos to generate electricity.[29]

4. Englishman Joseph Swan and American Thomas Edison in 1878-1879 invented the light bulb.[30]

5. Edison built a generating plant and an entire system of wires, switches, fuses and meters to light an entire building in Manhattan.[31]

6. Scottish Alexander Graham Bell invented the telephone in 1876.[32]

7. In the 1890s Nicola Tesla (Serbian but Accomplished in America) and American George Westinghouse introduced AC or Alternating Current.[33]

8. Swedish Alfred Nobel produced Dynamite in 1866.[34]

9. German Heinrich Hertz discovered electromagnetic waves other than light.[35]

10. In 1895 the German Wilhelm Roentgen discovered X-Rays.[36]

---

[29] 114
[30] 114-115
[31] 115
[32] 115
[33] 116
[34] 116
[35] 118
[36] 118

11. In 1895 Italian Guglielmo Marconi discovered "that electromagnetic waves could be used to transmit information...By 1899 he succeeded in sending a signal across the English Channel and two years later across the Atlantic Ocean."[37]

12. In 1859 the first internal combustion Engine was invented by Frenchman Etienne Lenoir.[38]

13. In 1883 German Karl Benz invented an internal combustion Engine that would operate in a vehicle.[39]

14. In 1896 American Henry Ford began to perfect the manufacture of the new Automobile, the Model T in 1908.[40]

15. In 1892 German Rudolph Diesel invented the Diesel Engine.[41]

16. In the early 20th century German Ferdinand von Zeppelin began to manufacture airships that were frequently used in Germany until the Hindenburg crashed in 1937.[42]

17. In 1903 the American Wright Brothers invented the first airplane.[43]

18. In 1945 Jewish American J. Robert Oppenheimer and his team built the first atom bomb.

---

[37] 118
[38] 119
[39] 119
[40] 119-120
[41] 120
[42] 120
[43] 120

19. In 1939 German Hans von Ohain built the first jet engine.[44]

20. German Konrad Zuse built the first digital computer. English Max Newman, and American Howard Aiken made considerable additions.[45]

21. Americans John Mauchly and J. Presper Eckert invented the first calculator.[46]

22. The first rocket was invented by German Werner von Braun.[47]

23. In 1928 Englishman Alexander Fleming invented antibiotics.

24. The Russians invented the first Nuclear Power plant in 1954 "followed by Calder Hall, Britain, in 1956".[48]

25. In 1957 the Russians[49] led by Sergei Korolev invented Sputnik.

26. In 1961 Russian Yuri Gagarin was the first cosmonaut.[50]

---

[44] 131
[45] 132
[46] 132
[47] 133
[48] 135
[49] 136
[50] 137

27. "In 1947-1948, Walter Brattain, William Shockley, and John Barden...created the first transistor".[51]

28. The Television was invented by the Scottish man John Baird. (The invention not the name was mentioned in the referenced Book)

29. In 1975 Stephen Wozniak and Steve Jobs "assembled their first computer circuit boards".[52]

30. In 1981 IBM purchased an operating system from a small software firm called Microsoft founded by Bill Gates and Paul Allen.[53]

31. In 1989 Englishman Tim Berners created the World Wide Web.[54]

32. In 1953 James Watson and Francis Crick "came up with the double-helix model of deoxyribonucleic acid, or DNA."[55]

33. In the 1950s the first Genetically Modified plant was invented by American Norman Borlaug.[56]

100% men and as a rule we are looking at white men from Protestant Countries. Not one woman is mentioned in this volume as having accomplished anything in the realm of civilization since her supposed liberation. Most of these men did all these

---

[51] 137
[52] 142
[53] 142
[54] 143
[55] 144
[56] 145

things when the Patriarchal Protestant Religion absolutely dominated the lives of men here and elsewhere in Europe and the British Isles. These men were generally raised up in homes where they were disciplined, the Fathers ruled the house, and the Bible was taught to them from their childhood. When you look at their pictures, you see men, with intense looks about their faces and they are dressed like Professionals. This was the manhood of possibly the greatest Gentile generations in world history. Today things are much different. The cultural archetypes of my generation, the wigger, the pothead, the punk-grunge and the sports-fan are all distinct modes of the same psychological nihilism that permeates the minds of the youth here in America. These young people have been taught to hate their Bible reading fathers, to hate their family's religion, to hate their history, and to firmly believe that things were never better in the past. The previous generation was raised to rule; the present generation is being raised to *serve* as subjects and slaves.

Pause

Thus, if women do not pull equal weight, if they do not have equal contributions to civilization, and if they do not have equal responsibilities in a society, as they don't and never will, they should not enjoy equal rights, privileges and franchise.

> *Luke 12:48 From everyone who has been given much, much will be required; and to whom they entrusted much, of him they will ask all the more.*

Moreover, these women have shown themselves incapable of choosing a qualified mate and raising a family as they have murdered over 50 million of their own children since Roe v. Wade.

The Sexual Revolution Was Based on Lies, Rape and Torture

Before the sexual revolution our country was an extraordinarily moral people being ruled by a Government that upheld many Biblical laws concerning sexual practice. Drs. Phyllis and Eberhard Kronhausen, state in a survey they conducted, *Sex Histories of American College Men*, (Ballantine Books, New York, 1960), p. 219,[57]

> "sex without love seemed utterly unethical. Some of them did not even think it right to kiss a girl unless they were "in love...In the college group as a whole one still finds considerable resistance toward premarital intercourse...premarital intercourse is considered highly objectionable for reasons which are primarily derived from religious tenets and beliefs and... overvaluation of virginity with particular respect to the female. This overvaluation of female virginity also prevails in the lower educational groups but there it is apparently not

---

[57] Judith Reisman, *Kinsey: Crimes and Consequences* (The Institute for Media Education, Inc., Crestwood, Kentucky, 2003), 101.

taken quite as seriously as in the upper educational groups.... [I]t remains a fact that this group engages in relatively little premarital sexual intercourse....

The average modern college man is apt to say that he considers intercourse "too precious" to have with anyone except the girl he expects to marry and may actually abstain from all intercourse for that reason."

This is completely contradictory to the modern Atheist and modern Christian theories of man that the world always has been a degenerate corrupt and perverted place and that no philosophy whatever, will ever make things better.

Due to the fraudulent data of Alfred Kinsey (Which will be proved later) men like Morris Ernst and David Loth argued in their *American Sexual Behavior and the Kinsey Report* pages 126-131 that these Biblical laws should be abrogated.

These changes were to be found in the Model Penal Code. Dr. Reisman states,

"According to Kinsey's authorized biographer, Jonathan Gathorne-Hardy, 'The American Law Institute's Model Penal Code of 1955 is virtually a Kinsey document.... At one point Kinsey is cited six times in twelve pages."[58]...

"Morris Ploscowe, one of the Model Penal Code's principal authors, argued--based on Kinsey's findings--that "When a total clean-up of sex offenders is demanded, it is in effect a proposal to put 95 percent of the male population in jail.... Of the total male population 85 per cent has had pre-marital intercourse...." Ploscowe introduced to the legal profession what Kinsey had certainly envisioned:

One of the conclusions of the Kinsey report is that the sex offender is not a monster... but an individual who is not very different from others in his social group, and that his behavior is similar to theirs. The only difference is that others in the offender's social group have not been apprehended. This recognition that there is nothing very shocking or abnormal in the sex offender's behavior should lead to other changes in sex legislation.... In the first place, it should lead to a downward revision of the penalties

---

[58] Reisman, 188, citing Jonathan Gathorne-Hardy, *Sex, Alfred C. Kinsey, The Measure of All Things*, (Chatto & Windus, London, 1998), 449.

presently imposed on sex offenders."[59]

Today, The Kinsey Institute promotes,

"XIII World Congress of Sexology Valencia Declaration on Sexual Rights...

We hereby urge that societies create the conditions to satisfy the needs for the full development of the individual and respect the following SEXUAL RIGHTS:

3. **The right to sexual equity and equality**. This refers to freedom from all forms of discrimination, paying due respect to sexual diversity, regardless of sex, gender, age, race, social class, religion and sexual orientation. ...

7. **The right to associate freely**. This means the possibility to marry or not, to divorce, and to establish other types of sexual associations."[60]

Reisman states,

---

[59] Reisman, 189, citing Morris Ploscowe, "Sexual Patterns and the Law," in *Sex Habits of American Men, A Symposium on the Kinsey Report* (Albert Deutsch, editor), Prentice Hall, New York, 1948, pp. 125-126, 133-134

[60] http://www.kinseyinstitute.org/resources/valencia.html

"In summary, the four 1948 Kinsey books, (1) Sex Habits of American Men: A Symposium on the Kinsey Report; (2) The Ethics of Sexual Acts; (3) About the Kinsey Report; and (4) American Sexual Behavior and the Kinsey Report; all say "thank you" to Kinsey for his legal aid in "educating juries and judges." The statement often repeated by Indiana University, Kinsey's employer, that Kinsey's "findings" were embargoed to media and scholars-at-large is refuted by these four complex books, released within a very few months of Kinsey's 1948 volume. Although he did not want to do so, Kinsey was expected to write the Female volume instead of his tome calling for a repeal of sex laws. However, these four books by legal and social science elitists launched the legal revolution better than Kinsey could have done himself as a mere zoologist. They, as academics, legal experts and scholars, spoke for Kinsey."[61]

Roe v. Wade cites Kinsey's work via the Model Penal Code. Linda Jeffrey, Ed.D. and Colonel Ronald D. Ray, J.D, state in their work *A History of the American Law Institutes Model Penal Code*,

"As 21st Century readers well know, when challenging American law, who

---

[61] Reisman,195-196

the judge is has become more important than what the law says. It is no coincidence that obscenity laws were being rewritten and a newly created zone of privacy was being established as a precedent to argue for the killing of the unborn. Here are some interesting facts discovered while researching the seven supreme Court Justices who agreed with Roe v. Wade and Doe v. Bolton on January 22, 1973—Harry Blackmun, (author of the opinion), Potter Stewart, William Douglas, Thurgood Marshall, William Brennan, Warren Burger, and Lewis Powell, and a few others who directly influenced their decisions.

Thomas Clark retired from the supreme Court in 1967, citing a conflict of interest with his son Ramsey Clark, who was appointed Attorney General. However, by the time Roe was decided in 1973, his vote was already cast in the abortion debate, with the publication of his article, *"Religion, Morality, and Abortion: A Constitutional Appraisal,"* in the Loyola University Law Review in 1969, which was cited by Blackmun in the Roe v. Wade opinion. Clark's stalwart hostility toward Christianity was recorded in the supreme Court opinion he wrote, Abington v. Schempp, 374 U.S. 203

(1963), which removed prayer and Bible reading from government schools."[62]

This citation can be read in Footnote 37 of Roe v. Wade – 410 U.S. 113 (1973).[63]

The Lies

The Kinsey Institute states,

"Sexual Behavior in the Human Male (1948) and Sexual Behavior in the Human Female (1953) reported that: 37% of males and 13% of females had at least some overt homosexual experience to orgasm; 10% of males were more or less exclusively

---

[62]http://www.drjudithreisman.com/archives/monograph_opt.pdf

[63] "[Footnote 37]
Fourteen States have adopted some form of the ALI statute. See Ark.Stat.Ann. §§ 41-303 to 41-310 (Supp. 1971); Calif.Health & Safety Code §§ 25950-25955.5 (Supp. 1972); Colo.Rev.Stat.Ann. §§ 40-2-50 to 40-2-53 (Cum.Supp. 1967); Del.Code Ann., Tit. 24, §§ 1790-1793 (Supp. 1972); Florida Law of Apr. 13, 1972, c. 72-196, 1972 Fla.Sess.Law Serv., pp. 380-382; Ga.Code §§ 26-1201 to 26-1203 (1972); Kan.Stat.Ann. § 21-3407 (Supp. 1971); Md.Ann.Code, Art. 43, §§ 137-139 (1971); Miss.Code Ann. § 2223 (Supp. 1972); N.M.Stat.Ann. §§ 40A-5-1 to 40A-5-3 (1972); N.C.Gen.Stat. § 14-45.1 (Supp. 1971); Ore.Rev.Stat. §§ 435.405 to 435.495 (1971); S.C.Code Ann. §§ 16-82 to 16-89 (1962 and Supp. 1971); Va.Code Ann. §§ 18.1-62 to 18.1-62.3 (Supp. 1972). Mr. Justice Clark described some of these States as having "led the way." Religion, Morality, and Abortion: A Constitutional Appraisal, 2 Loyola U. (L.A.) L.Rev. 1, 11 (1969)." http://supreme.justia.com/cases/federal/us/410/113/case.html#F37

homosexual and 8% of males were exclusively homosexual for at least three years between the ages of 16 and 55. For females, Kinsey reported a range of 2-6% for more or less exclusively homosexual experience/response. 4% of males and 1-3% of females had been exclusively homosexual after the onset of adolescence up to the time of the interview. Kinsey devised a classification scheme to measure sexual orientation. It is commonly known as the Kinsey Scale".[64]…

"69% of white males have had at least one experience with a prostitute"[65]…

"Males: Kinsey estimated that approximately 50% of all married males had some extramarital experience at some time during their married lives (p. 585, 587, Male)."[66]…

"Extramarital Sex Incidence

Males: Kinsey estimated that approximately 50% of all married males had some extramarital

---

[64] http://www.iub.edu/~kinsey/resources/bib-homoprev.html
[65] http://www.kinseyinstitute.org/research/ak-data.html
[66] http://www.kinseyinstitute.org/research/ak-data.html#extramaritalcoitus

experience at some time during their married lives (p. 585, 587, Male).

Females: Among the sample, 26% of females had had extramarital sex by their forties. Between 1 in 6 and 1 in 10 females from age 26 to 50 were engaged in extramarital sex, (p. 416, Female).”…

“Premarital Sex

Occurs in:

Males: 67-98%, depending on socioeconomic level. 68% by age 18 had experienced premarital coitus, (p. 549-52, and Table 136, p. 550, Male).

Females: about 50%, (p. 286, and Table 75, p. 333 and Table 79, p. 337, Female).”[67]

Reisman states,

“Among the 62 groups for which Kinsey claimed to have collected 100 percent samples, Terman counted “four delinquent groups, two penal groups, and one group in a 'mental' institution… three classes of junior high school students… three rooming-house groups, two groups of conscientious objectors and a group

---

[67] http://www.kinseyinstitute.org/research/ak-data.html

of hitchhikers." He notes that "it is unlikely that[these men were] representative of the U.S."[68]

The Kinsey Team's Estimated 86 percent Aberrant Sample in *Male* Numbers	
Aberrant Population	**Estimated Sample**
Prison Sex Offenders and Psychopaths (documented above)	1,600
Prison Non-Sex Offenders (documented above)	329
Experimental Child Subjects (Chapter 7, at minimum)	317
Experimental School Boys (Chapter 7, at minimum)	350
"Pimps, Thieves, Ne'er-do-wells" (Kinsey's terms), etc.	300
Homosexuals	630
Total Aberrant Population	*3,526*
– Roughly 86 percent of the 4,120 Male Population were Sexual Deviants	

Paul Gebhard admits in the documentary *One in Ten: The Kinsey Percentage by* Madelene Pretorius, Manhattan Center Studios, around the 21 minute mark that 55% of the less than college-educated male sample were prisoners.[69]

This sophistry also plays a role in the abortion data in Volume 3. Remember, in the *Female Volume*, page 53, Kinsey defined a married woman as a woman who had merely cohabited with a man for at least a year. That would not have been

---

[68] Reisman, 97, citing, Louis Terman, "Kinsey's Sexual Behavior in the Human Male: Some Comments and Criticisms," *Psychological Bulletin* 45, 1948, 447
[69] *http://www.youtube.com/watch?v=wJtVzDTjPs4*

representative of the US population's idea of marriage. Now to Volume 3:

On page xi we see that the data of the Kinsey Institute was of "immediate importance" to the participants of a Planned Parenthood Conference in 1955, and on page xiii that Kinsey's work was the Foundation for Volume 3 of the Kinsey Institute and Gebhard reminds us of "the debt science and society in general owe to Dr. Kinsey". On page 14 we read that the sample from which data was received by the Kinsey institute was a highly irregular sample. It states that the women involved in this study were, "made up of persons who had some interest in, and comprehended the value of, sex research". Most American women at this time would not have been interested in divulging their most intimate sexual experiences with total strangers. On page 16 we read that 58 per cent of his sample were unmarried and "of those who did marry, a relatively large number were subsequently separated, divorced, or widowed" along with many common law marriages. Yet at this time "Eighty-two percent of the female population in 1950 was married (out of non-widows between the ages of 18 and 64)".[70]

Thus, the Kinsey data is the foundation for the modern Abortion movement and that data given by the Kinsey institute is clearly skewed. We are then faced with a huge conspiracy.

The Rape and Torture

---

[70] http://www.nber.org/papers/w10772.pdf?new_window=1

In the Male Volume, page 161 Kinsey stated that sobbing, groaning, crying, fainting, fear, pain and collapsing are a part of an orgasm, indicating evidence of rape and of Kinsey's pedophile and/or sadomasochist tendencies as if that had happened to himself. Kinsey states that the subject will "fight away from the partner and may make violent attempts to avoid climax". Page 177 states that Kinsey employed 9 adult male subjects to calculate the data from such experiences. On page 180 we see that a child had 26 orgasms in 24 hours evidencing clear torture.

In the Female Volume, page 53 we see that the Kinsey group defined a married woman as a woman who had cohabitated with a man for at least a year. This was clearly a misrepresentation of what marriage meant to the US population in the mid 20th century. On page 83 we see that the Kinsey group prepared these pedophile rapists to calculate their activities and on page 84 that they were "urged to write us for instructions." Page 86 and 88 admits that their data was based, at least in part, on the activities of prison inmates.

Secret History was a long-running British television documentary series. In *Secret History: Kinsey's Paedophiles* in their interview with Paul Gebhard, Gebhard admits at the 31-33 minute mark,

> "That was rather easy. We got them in prisons, a lot of them.... We'd go after them.... Then there was also a paedophile organization in this country... not incarcerated...they

cooperated... You had one in Britain...
a British paedophile organization."[71]

Gebhard admits, November 2, 1992, in his telephone interview with J. Gordon Muir, M.D., that the persons doing the timing were "parents at our suggestion"! Then immediately admits to suggesting the same thing to "nursery school personnel". J. Gordon Muir, M.D., asked Gebhard how the experimenters and observers just happened to have stopwatches to so accurately record the exact time these children were orgasmic. Gebhard says, "they do if that we tell them that we're interested in it."[72]

The Kinsey Institute acknowledged the allegations made also by Esther White,

> "The 'Esther White' allegations: In a British documentary, from 1998, a woman says she was sexually abused by her father and grandfather, and that her father justified it as doing research for Alfred Kinsey by filling out questionnaires, and claimed he was paid by Kinsey for abusing his daughter."[73]

In *Secret History: Kinsey's Paedophiles'* (1998) director, Tim Tate stated that Esther White and her mother swore a Statutory Declaration that what she said was true before she was interviewed for the documentary.[74]

---

[71] http://www.youtube.com/watch?v=UVC-1d5ib50
[72] *The Kinsey Syndrome*, 1:08
[73] http://www.kinseyinstitute.org/about/controversy2.html
[74] *The Kinsey Syndrome*, 1:17

Is it then any surprise that our laws have been changed to protect sexual predators at the expense of women and children? The UK Center for Research on Violence Against Women's *Top ten things advocates need to know* article states that "A national study estimates only 37% of reported rapes are prosecuted" and of those only "18% of prosecuted rape cases end in a conviction"![75]

And guess what? Atheist apologists and modern young people will blame God for all of this! Yet God revealed to man sexual laws and principles and ordained institutions that this country generally followed until 50 years ago and these laws produced a very moral society as has been proved. This country, following Ernst and Loth, rejected Yah's laws and principles and opened the gates of hell upon themselves, (and folks these sexual issues are only the beginning) and then they have the nerve to turn around and blame God? Unbelievable! Reader if you ever come across a young person or a Feminist who is bitter at God for some terrible thing that has happened in their past, do not let them manipulate you! Ask them some basic questions: 1. Do you believe that the slavery institution is a sin? 2. Do you believe in racial equality? 3. Do you believe in gender equality? 4. Do you believe that people are free to think and act as they please as long as they don't physically harm someone else? If yes, then all of this chaos that you are living in is your Reconstruction Fantasy come true, and you have no

_____

[75]http://www.uky.edu/CRVAW/files/TopTen/07_Rape_Prosec ution.pdf

one to blame but yourself! This is what you wanted! You are getting exactly what you deserve!

> *Isa. 3:10 Say to the righteous that it will go well with them, For they will eat the fruit of their actions.11 Woe to the wicked! It will go badly with him, For what he deserves will be done to him.*

The Disastrous Effects of Women's Suffrage and Sexual "Liberation"

In 1962 Hugh Heffner published *The Playboy Philosophy*. In it he cites Kinsey's work numerous times to justify the need for his explicit literature. [76] Thus, Kinsey's work is the basis for the modern Pornography industry and if it can be proven that there is a correlation between pornography and the sex trafficking industry, the basis for the modern sex slave trade. Reisman catalogs the change in the following documents which you can read for free online:

---

[76] http://brentdanley.com/wp-content/uploads/2007/04/theplayboyphilosophy.pdf

Scientific Authority for the Sex Industrial Complex (SIC) in the 20th - 21st Century

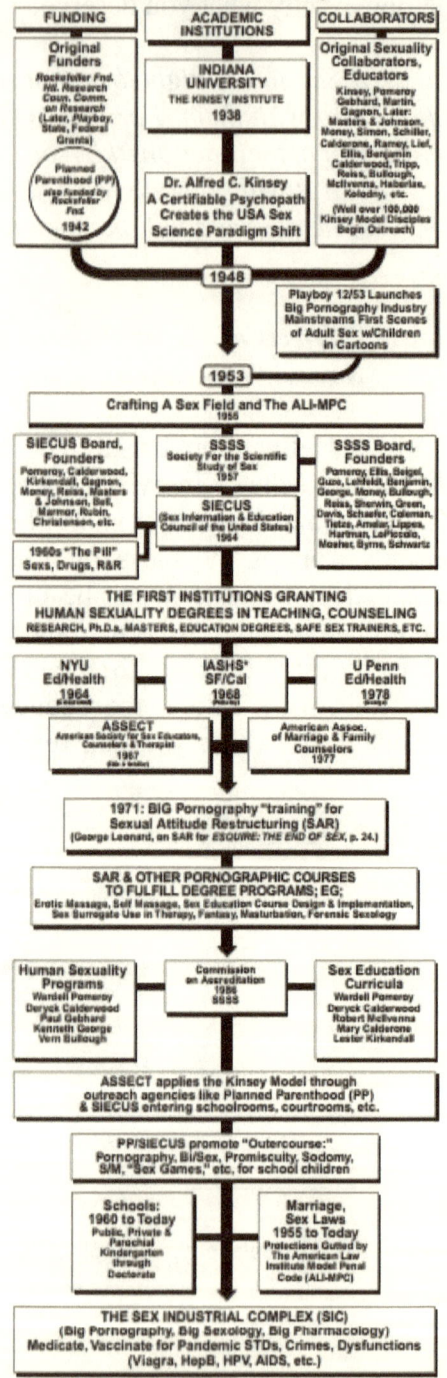

46

THE MODEL PENAL CODE (MPC) REMOVES PROTECTIONS FOR WOMEN & CHILDREN
U.S. Justice System 1948 - Today: Experts Usurp Jury of One's Peers

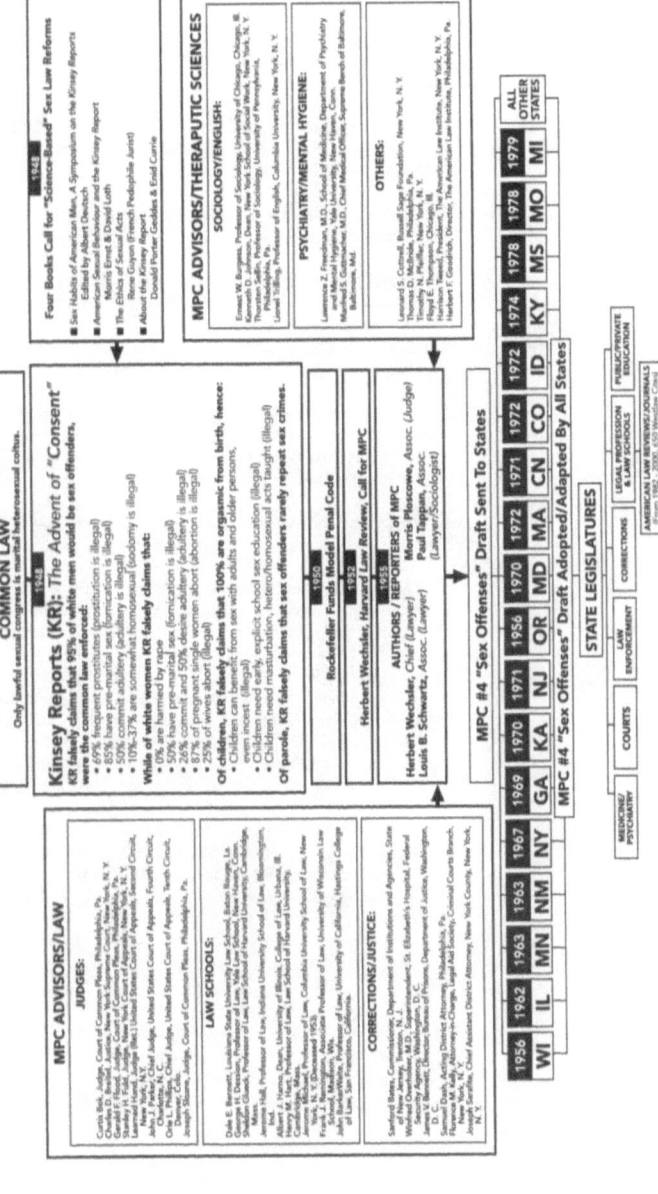

PRE-1948
COMMON LAW
Only lawful sexual congress is marital heterosexual coitus.

1948
Four Books Call for "Science-Based" Sex Law Reforms
- Sex Habits of American Men, A Symposium on the Kinsey Reports
  Edited by Albert Deutsch
- American Sexual Behavior and the Kinsey Report
  Morris Ernst & David Loth
- The Ethics of Sexual Acts
  Rene Guyon (French Pedophile Jurist)
- About the Kinsey Report
  Donald Porter Geddes & Enid Curtie

Kinsey Reports (KR): The Advent of "Consent"
KR falsely claims that 95% of white men would be sex offenders, were the common law enforced:
- 69% frequent prostitutes (prostitution is illegal)
- 85% have pre-marital sex (fornication is illegal)
- 50% commit adultery (adultery is illegal)
- 10%-37% are somewhat homosexual (sodomy is illegal)

While of white women KR falsely claims that:
- 0% are harmed by rape
- 50% have pre-marital sex (fornication is illegal)
- 26% commit and 50% desire adultery (adultery is illegal)
- 87% of pregnant single women abort (abortion is illegal)
- 25% of women abort (abortion is illegal)

Of children, KR falsely claims that 100% are orgasmic from birth, hence:
- Children can benefit from sex with adults and older persons, even incest (illegal)
- Children need early, explicit school sex education (illegal)
- Children need masturbation, hetero/homosexual acts taught (illegal)

Of parole, KR falsely claims that sex offenders rarely repeat sex crimes.

1950
Rockefeller Funds Model Penal Code

1952
Herbert Wechsler, Harvard Law Review, Call for MPC

1955
AUTHORS / REPORTERS of MPC
Herbert Wechsler, Chief (Lawyer)   Morris Ploscowe, Assoc. (Judge)
Louis B. Schwartz, Assoc. (Lawyer)   Paul Tappan, Assoc.
                                      (Lawyer/Sociologist)

MPC #4 "Sex Offenses" Draft Sent To States

WI	IL	MN	NM	NY	GA	KA	OR	NJ	MD	MA	CN	CO	ID	KY	MS	MO	MI	ALL OTHER STATES
1956	1962	1963	1963	1967	1969	1970	1971	1971	1970	1972	1971	1972	1972	1974	1978	1978	1979	

MPC #4 "Sex Offenses" Draft Adopted/Adapted By All States

STATE LEGISLATURES

MPC ADVISORS/LAW

JUDGES:

LAW SCHOOLS:

CORRECTIONS/JUSTICE:

MPC ADVISORS/THERAPUTIC SCIENCES

SOCIOLOGY/ENGLISH:

PSYCHIATRY/MENTAL HYGIENE:

OTHERS:

MEDICINE/PSYCHIATRY | COURTS | LAW ENFORCEMENT | CORRECTIONS | LEGAL PROFESSION & LAW SCHOOLS | PUBLIC/PRIVATE EDUCATION

AMERICAN LAW REVIEWS/JOURNALS
(From 1982 - 2000, 650 WestLaw Cites)

A General Overview of How State Criminal Code Reform Proceeded
Largely during the 60s and 70s is as follows:

1. After the 1952 call in the Harvard Law Review by Professor Herbert Wechsler, the American Law Institute's Model Penal Code (Draft #4) was distributed to the states in 1955.

2..The state legislature provides funding, with federal assistance in some instances through the 1968 Omnibus Crime Control and Safe Streets Act, to form a Commission to reform/revise the state criminal code. The Commission advises and approves drafts written by one or more "reporting staff."

3. The Commission consisted of law school professors from each major law school, judges, and prosecutors. Some states had advisory committees that included the therapeutic sciences, and corrections.

4. The Commission and/or drafting committee examines the American Law Institute Model Penal Code as its primary source for reform including the ALI's recommended changes. There is also frequent reference to the early state revisions in Illinois (1962), New York (1967) and New Jersey (1971). Some states also looked at the Louisiana laws which are uniquely based on the Napoleonic code. There are specific citations to The Kinsey Reports, as well as the Wolfenden Report (a study of Sodomy in Great Britain) in the sex offenses recommendations, or to "second generation" sources which cite to The Kinsey Reports via the 1955 draft of the MPC being a primary example.

5. The Commission or one of its key spokesmen publishes an article calling for "reform" in a law school or Bar journal. The justification given is that existing law is "obsolete," not based on "current social and scientific thought," and too complex. Some cite examples such as references to trains and livery stables.

6. In the "Crimes against the person" and "offenses against morals" state law code sections, are renamed "sex offenses" in the Model Penal Code.

7. The common law concept of "consent" primarily to marry (or to determine if the crime was rape or fornication) is twisted to move toward legalization of all sexual contacts between "consenting adults," with the age of consent being lowered in most cases.

8. Forcible rape becomes so narrowly defined by the requirement that the victim prove her resistance by injury or death, that the lesser crimes or infractions are often plea-bargained. One state (Minnesota) has eliminated the term "rape" all together. Others use "sexual assault," "sexual misconduct," "sexual contact," "sexual conduct," "illegal intercourse," or other terms to describe sex offenses. The new terms for rape in the reformed codes are defined differently from state to state, as are the ages applied, and the penalties.

9. The state revision Commission introduces the concept of "forcible compulsion" into the definition of rape (burden of proof shifts from the predator to the victim), and the crime is diminished by the creation of lesser offenses based on degree of non consent, the age of the victim, and age differential of the offender and victim, the amount of injury, the relationship between the predator and victim, if any.

10. As recommended by the Model Penal Code and The Kinsey Reports (Male Volume p. 392), the age of consent is moved to between 12 and 16, and offenses are graded downward as the age of the victim increases.

11. Generally, the state and common laws protecting marriage are abolished or penalties reduced. For example, consensual fornication, adultery, and sodomy are legal in many states. Bestiality and necrophilia are eliminated or moved from the sex offenses section to "cruelty to animals" or "abuse of a corpse."

12. The new criminal law code is presented to the state legislature as "merely technical improvement" without major substantive change, and is passed in whole or significant part.

CAUSAL EFFECT OF KINSEY'S FRAUDULENT "DATA"

THE 1955 AMERICAN LAW INSTITUTE "MODEL PENAL CODE" ELIMINATES COMMON LAW TO REDUCE/END SEX OFFENSE LAWS AND PAROLE ALL CRIMINALS

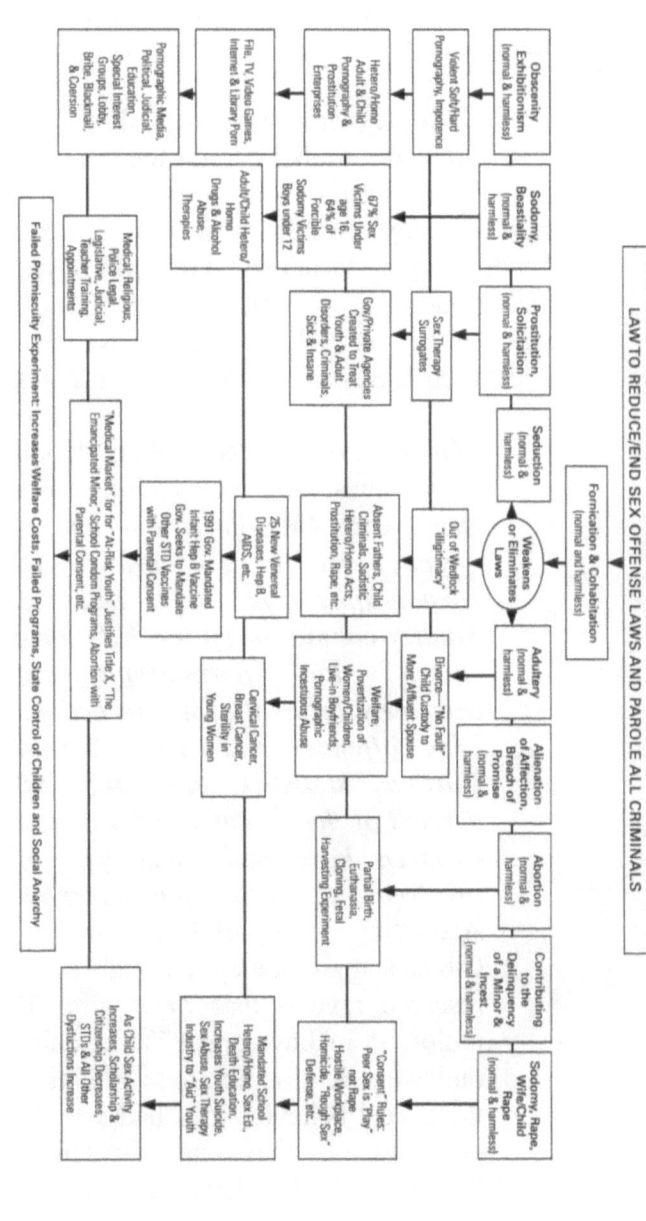

49

Here then is the plague of modern man's liberation and his own wisdom. Nambla even roots itself in Kinsey's work.[77]

Statutes like Jessica's law, the Adam Walsh Act, Carlie's Law, the Amber Alert, Megan's Law and the Jimmy Ryce Act all testify to the deviant nature of America today. Just do a Google search on Sex offenders in your local neighborhood and you will be shocked and what we have become. California Law Firm Estey & Bomberger's website Child Molestation & Sexual Abuse Statistics states,

> "The number of victims of childhood sexual abuse and molestation grows each year. ***This horrific crime is directly tied to the growth of pornography on the Internet. Studies conducted by the FBI have shown that pornography is extremely influential in the actions of sex offenders and serial murders. Further, statistics show that 90 percent of the predators who molest children have had some type of involvement with pornography***. According to Charles Keating of Citizens for Decency Through Law, research reveals that 77% of child molesters of boys and 87% of child molesters of girls admitted imitating the sexual behavior they had seen in pornography they had watched. Roughly 33% of girls and 14% of

---

[77] http://nambla.org/kinsey.html

boys are molested before the age of 18, according to the U.S. Justice Department. Nearly 2/3 of all sexual assaults reported involved minors and roughly 1/3 involved children under the age of 12. In most cases, however, child molestation goes unreported. Estimates are that only 35% of sexual abuse is reported. Kids can be frightened or embarrassed and many times do not say anything."[78]

According to the Center for Disease Control and Prevention, *Trends in Reportable Sexually Transmitted Diseases in the United States*, 2007, National Surveillance Data for Chlamydia, Gonorrhea, and Syphilis, in the United States, "19 million new infections occur each year".[79] According to the New York Times, Health Guide, "Current trends project that 1 in 3 American women will be sexually assaulted at some point during her life."[80] The FBI estimates that 300, 000 young people are sex slaves in the US.[81] According to the *Trafficking in Persons Report*, U.S. Department of State, "It is estimated that as many as 27 million men, women, and children around the world are victims of what is now often described with the umbrella term "human trafficking."[82]

---

[78] http://www.childmolestationvictim.com/child-molestation-sexual-abuse-statistics/
[79] http://www.cdc.gov/std/stats07/trends.htm
[80]http://health.nytimes.com/health/guides/specialtopic/rape/overview.html?inline=nyt-classifier
[81] http://www.fbi.gov/stats-services/publications/law-enforcement-bulletin/march_2011/human_sex_trafficking
[82] http://www.state.gov/documents/organization/192587.pdf, 7

And who are the people buying these sex slaves? Mostly men addicted to hard core porn as we saw above from Estey & Bomberger.

When exploiting one of these sex slaves, the predator will tape it and make a porno out of it. According to the European Online Grooming Project, *March 2012 Final Report – Executive Summary*, which deals with sexual abuse via the internet,

> "The relative ease in which illegal content could be sourced was an important maintaining feature – some [Sexual predators, a.k.a. "online groomers"-DS] talked about viewing pornography and indecent images as a normal part of their life. The scale of indecent material available online also had a bearing on some behaviours - with so much material online to view, groomers do not feel isolated or 'different' viewing the content."[83]

Again, according to the European Online Grooming Project,

> "As well as maintaining or supporting online sexual offending, for some online groomers viewing adult pornography and indecent images of children was discussed as having a

---

[83] http://www.europeanonlinegroomingproject.com/wp-content/file-uploads/European-Online-Grooming-Project-Executive-Summary.pdf, 9

role in escalating deviant behaviour by:

o Saturation: some men did not become so easily aroused when masturbating to a particular type of image. Consequently they moved from images they saw as mild to material that was ever more explicit and thus arousing again.

o Denial of harm to child: the features of some images were focused on to justify and
continue offending, such as those showing the young person smiling.

o Fantasy: indecent images helped 'bring to life' the young person being groomed online. For example, one participant talked about asking a young person to describe themselves in detail so he could quickly match that description to an indecent image. The image was then used during masturbation whilst concurrently chatting to the young person.

o Demand fuelling status: as well as meeting individual needs, there was also kudos and credibility in being a provider of indecent image material. In turn, this made some individuals feel important and so want to create and share more images of abuse..."[84]

According to the OECD Family Database, *SF2.4: Share of births out of wedlock and teenage births*, the United States has a 40% illegitimacy rate.[85]

According to Legal Momentum, The Women's Legal Defense and Education Fund, *Single Motherhood in the United States – A Snapshot (2012)*, half of American mothers will spend some time as the single custodian of a child![86]

The pill was first made legal here in 1960 but Eisenstadt v. Baird, 405 U.S. 438 (1972), a United States Supreme Court case, established the right of unmarried people to possess contraception on the same basis as married couples and thus, by implication, the right of unmarried couples to engage in nonprocreative sexual intercourse. The children produced from these selfish relationships are generally unwanted. According to the Guttmacher Institute, *Facts on Induced Abortion In the United States*, 53 million abortions have been performed in America since Roe V. Wade.[87] This genocide is unforgivable and the Politicians, doctors, nurses, educators and activists who have performed or advocated for this evil should be given a Dilation and Evacuation by the Civil Magistrate after being

---

[84] Ibid., 12-14
[85]http://www.oecd.org/social/familiesandchildren/40278615.pdf
[86] http://www.legalmomentum.org/our-work/women-and-poverty/resources--publications/single-mothers-snapshot.pdf
[87] http://www.guttmacher.org/pubs/fb_induced_abortion.html

convicted in a Court of Law.[88] As they have done so shall it be done to them. Their penalty should be death by torture. They should be ripped limb from limb with a "grasping instrument (forceps)...to grasp larger pieces of tissue."

> *Exo. 21: 23 But if there is any further injury, then you shall appoint as a penalty life for life, 24 eye for eye, tooth for tooth, hand for hand, foot for foot, 25 burn for burn, wound for wound, bruise for bruise.*

And yet we are to believe that in ***traditional*** marriage people are abused!!!!! Isn't that just precious? Margret Sanger developed the pill to liberate women from the "tyranny" of pregnancy. Once sex was disconnected from pregnancy, the old bargain, sex for marriage (physical and emotional stability-life long companionship) collapsed. What then have women got to offer? Not only do they have nothing to offer in exchange for life-long companionship, the fact that women now have sex with so many men, drives men even further from committing to a woman many of his friends have already had sex with. This leaves women mostly single as they ascend into their later years, bitter, and alone.

Feminist women will demand that these consequences are the inevitable results of equality. That is true, and the Christian Pastors, in their fear and cowardice refuse to face the root issue: men and women are not equal and they never will be.

---

[88] http://women.webmd.com/dilation-and-evacuation-de-for-abortion

The Bible's Teaching on Gender Relations

Supremacy and Subordination

Principles of supremacy and subordination are ultimately grounded in the relationship between the Father and the Son. Like nature does not imply absolute equality. Parents and children are both human but they are not equals. Magistrates and citizens are both human but they are not equals. Employers and employees are both human but they are not equals.

> *John 14:28 "You heard me say, 'I am going away and I am coming back to you.' If you loved me, you would be glad that I am going to the Father, for the Father is greater than I.*

Paul Makes The Same Argument That The Subordination Of Women Is Not Arbitrary But Ontologically Based In Their Origin In Man Just Like The Son's Subordination To The Father

> *1 Tim 2:11 A woman must quietly receive instruction with entire submissiveness. 12 But I do not allow a woman to teach or exercise authority over a man, but to remain quiet. 13 **For it was Adam who was first created, and then Eve**. 14 And it was not Adam who was deceived, but the woman being deceived, fell into transgression.*

1 Cor. 11: 3: "The head of the woman is the man."

1 Cor. 14:34: " Let your women keep silence in the churches, for it is not permitted unto them to speak; but they are commanded to be under obedience, as also saith the law."

Eph. 5:22-24: "Wives, submit yourselves unto your own husbands, as unto the Lord, for the husband is the Therefore as the church is subject unto Christ, so let the wives be to their own husbands in everything."

1 Tim. 2: 11-12: "Let the woman learn in silence, with all subjection. But I suffer not a woman to teach nor to usurp authority over the man, but to be in silence"

1 Tim. 5:14: "I will, therefore, that the younger women marry, bear children, guide the house, give none occasion to the adversary to speak reproachfully."

Titus, 2: 4-5: "That they may teach the young women to be sober, to love their husbands, to love their children, to be discreet, chaste, keepers at home, good, obedient to their own husbands, that the word of God be not blasphemed."

1 Pet. 3: 1, 5, 6: "Likewise, ye wives, be in subjection to your own husbands, that if any obey not the word they also without the word may be won by the conversation of the wives; for after this manner in the old time the holy women also, who trusted in God, adorned themselves, being in subjection to their own husbands, even as Sarah obeyed Abraham, calling him lord."

Gen. 3:16 To the woman He said, "I will greatly multiply Your pain in childbirth, In pain you will bring forth children; Yet your desire will be for your husband, And he will rule over you."

Num. 30: 1 Then Moses spoke to the heads of the tribes of the sons of Israel, saying, "This is the word which the Lord has commanded. 2 If a man makes a vow to the Lord, or takes an oath to bind himself with a binding obligation, he shall not violate his word; he shall do according to all that proceeds out of his mouth. 3 "Also if a woman makes a vow to the Lord, and binds herself by an obligation in her father's house in her youth, 4 and her father hears her vow and her obligation by which she has bound herself, and her father says nothing to her, then all her vows shall stand and every obligation by which she has bound herself shall stand. 5 But if her father should forbid her on the day he hears of it, none of her vows or her obligations by which she has bound herself shall stand; and the Lord will forgive her because her father had forbidden her.6 "However, if she should marry while under her vows or the rash statement of her lips by which she has bound herself,7 and her husband hears of it and says nothing to her on the day he hears it, then her vows shall stand and her obligations by which she has bound herself shall stand. 8 But if on the day her husband hears of it, he forbids her, then he shall annul her vow which she is under and the rash statement of her lips by which she has bound herself; and the Lord will forgive her. 9 "But the vow of a widow or of a divorced woman, everything by which she has bound herself, shall stand against her.10 However, if she vowed in her husband's house, or bound herself by an obligation with an oath, 11 and her husband heard it, but said nothing to her and did not forbid her, then all her vows shall stand and every obligation by which she bound herself shall stand. 12 But if her husband indeed annuls them on the day he hears them, then whatever proceeds out of her lips concerning her vows or concerning the obligation of herself shall not stand; her husband has annulled them, and the Lord will forgive her.13 "Every vow and every binding oath to humble herself, her husband may confirm it or her husband may annul it. 14 But if her husband indeed says nothing to her from day to day, then he confirms all her vows or all her obligations which are on her; he has confirmed them, because he said nothing to her on the day he heard them. 15 But if he indeed annuls them after he has heard them, then he shall bear her guilt."

Men have a superiority over all women with reference to privileges and franchise. Men are the ones who have their blood shed and their bodies broken for the maintaining of civilization and men are the ones who have and continue to invent the most important devices in modern technology. Thus, the rule that Scripture sets down is in front of us on a daily basis and only pathological liars, devoted to the downfall of the Protestant Reformation, deny it.

Head Coverings

1 Cor. 11:1 Be imitators of me, just as I also am of Christ. 2 Now I praise you because you remember me in everything and hold firmly to the traditions, just as I delivered them to you. 3 But I want you to understand that Christ is the head of every man, and the man is the head of a woman, and God is the head of Christ. 4 Every man who has something on his head while praying or prophesying disgraces his head. 5 But every woman who has her head uncovered while praying or prophesying disgraces her head, for she is one and the same as the woman whose head is shaved. 6 For if a woman does not cover her head, let her also have her hair cut off; but if it is disgraceful for a woman to have her hair cut off or her head shaved, let her cover her head. 7 For a man ought not to have his head covered, since he is the image and glory of God; but the woman is the glory of man. 8 For man does not originate from woman, but woman from man; 9 for indeed man was not created for the woman's sake, but woman for the man's sake. 10 Therefore the woman ought to have a symbol of authority on her head, because of the angels. 11 However, in the Lord, neither is woman independent of man, nor is man independent of woman. 12 For as the woman originates from the man, so also the man has his birth through the woman; and all things originate from God. 13 Judge for yourselves: is it proper for a woman to pray to God with her head uncovered? 14 Does not even nature itself teach you that if a man has long hair, it is a dishonor to him, 15 but if a woman has long *hair, it is a glory to her? For her hair is given to her for a covering. 16 But if one is inclined to be contentious, we have no other practice, nor have the churches of God.*

17 But in giving this instruction, I do not praise you, because you come together not for the better but for the worse. 18 For, in the first place, when you come together as a church, I hear that divisions exist among you; and in part I believe it. 19 For there must also be factions among you, so that those who are approved may become evident among you. 20 Therefore when you meet together, it is not to eat the Lord's Supper, 21 for in your eating each one takes his own supper first; and one is hungry and another is drunk. 22 What! Do you not have houses in which to eat and drink? Or do you despise the church of God and shame those who have nothing? What shall I say to you? Shall I praise you? In this I will not praise you.

Head Coverings in Public Worship by Brian Schwertley states,

"The contrast that Paul sets up between men and women in v. 5 is even clearer than v. 4. Here the apostle uses the phrase "having her head uncovered" or literally "unveiled." The Greek word in all its various forms used throughout this section (e.g., v. 5, akatakalupto- "unveiled"; v. 6, ou katakaluptetai- "is not veiled"; v. 6, katakaluptestho- "let her be veiled"; v. 7, ouk opheilei katakaluptesthai- "ought not to be veiled"; v. 13, akatakalupton- "unveiled") clearly refers to a cloth covering or veil.

This interpretation is supported by the Septuagint (i.e., the Greek translation of the Old Testament completed in 247 B. C.), which used the various forms of katakalupte to describe a fabric of cloth covering. In Geneses 38:4-15 the same word (ekalupisato , katekalupato) is used to describe Tamar covering herself with a veil. It is obvious that it does not refer to a hair covering. In Isaiah 47:2-3 we read: "Take the millstones and grind meal. Remove your veil (apokilupsai to katakalumma), take off the skirt (anakalupsai tas polias).... Your nakedness shall be uncovered (anakaluphthesetai). Once again the covering is cloth or fabric.

The word akaluptos or covering is derived from the word kalumma, which means a veil. Regarding kalumma Greg Price writes: "This word is used some eighteen times in the Greek Old Testament (Ex. 26:14; 27:16; 34:33, 34, 35; 39:20; 40:5;

Num. 3:25; 4:8, 10, 11, 12, 14 twice, 25 twice, 31; 1 Chron. 17:5). In all of its uses in the Greek Old Testament and in the Greek New Testament (2 Cor. 3:13, 14, 15, 16), it never refers to hair as a veil but always to a fabric veil. Thus, when seeking to identify the nature of the veil that covered the head or the veil that is to be removed from the head, unless the context specifically designates kalumma (or one of its derivatives) to be the hair (which is never the case), it ought to be assumed that the veil referred to is a fabric veil worn over the hair.

Second, the covering of a man's head is associated with shame by the apostle Paul. The background of this assertion is the Old Testament where in times of sorrow or when men experienced shame they covered their heads with a cloth covering. In 2 Samuel 15:30 we read: "So David went up by the Ascent of the Mount of Olives, and wept as he went up; and he had his head covered and went barefoot. And all the people who were with him covered their heads and went up, weeping as they went up" (cf. Esther 6:12). "Another instance of the Hebrew word is in Jeremiah 14: 3-4, when men are ashamed and confounded, and covered their heads, because of a dearth brought by God's judgment. The only other Old

Testament occurrence of this word in the grammatical Qal stem is in Ester 7:8; it would seem that in each of these Old Testament events an external cloth covering is what is in view.

Third, the idea that the covering refers to hair and not a cloth veil is rendered impossible by Paul's comparison between being uncovered and having short mannish hair. In verse 5 the apostle says that being uncovered is bad because it is shameful like having short hair (i.e., shorn or shaven). It would be absurd for Paul to say that it is wrong or shameful for a woman to have short hair in public worship because having short hair is like having short hair. Note further what the apostle says in verse 6: "For if a woman is not covered, let her also be shorn." Would it make sense for Paul to say, "If a woman has short hair, then let her also have short hair"? No, not at all! The apostle is saying that if a woman is going to appear in church without a veil or cloth covering which is shameful then she might as well cut her hair short like a slave or lesbian. The apostle's analogy only makes sense if he is comparing one shameful activity to another shameful act. If both activities are identical, then the whole analogy is nonsense. Some Christians have attempted to circumvent this analogy by defining shorn and shaven in two different manners: one meaning short hair, while the other pointing to a bald head. This argument falls to the ground when we observe the fact that Paul uses the terms as synonyms in verse 6: "shorn or shaved." The covering can only refer to a cloth or veil; hair simply does not and cannot work in this context.

Fourth, in verse seven Paul says that man is not to be covered because "he is the image and glory of God; but the woman is the glory of man." Thus, the woman must be covered. Only God's glory is to be uncovered during the service. In verse 15 we are told that a woman's long hair is her glory. Since only God's glory is to be uncovered during public worship the woman's glory must be covered. "The hair of a woman cannot be both the glory and that which covers the glory! Nothing can be both 'A' and 'non-A' at the same time and in the same way. Paul taught us that the object which is the glory cannot also cover the glory! And he taught us that only God's glory is to be seen in the worship service." Obviously then, the woman's glory (i.e., her long hair) must be covered with a cloth fabric of some kind...

There is one common objection to all the proceeding arguments. It usually takes the form of a question. Doesn't Paul explicitly say in verse 15 that her hair is given to "her for a covering"? In other words, why should a woman wear a veil for a covering when Paul says that long hair is her covering? There are a number of reasons why long hair could not be the covering that Paul requires throughout this chapter. As noted, the meaning of the word for covering used in verses 4, 5, 6, 7 and 13 clearly refers to a cloth covering or veil in Scripture. Interestingly, when the apostle refers to long hair as a covering he uses a completely different Greek word (paribolain) in order to distinguish one type of head covering from another. "The fact Paul consistently uses different forms of kalumma (katakalupto, akatakaluptos, akatakalupto) in 1 Corinthians when referring to the veil to be worn in worship, but suddenly introduces peribolaion when referring to the natural covering of the hair, strongly urges that a distinction is being drawn between two different kinds of head coverings. Why introduce a different word if not to distinguish one head covering from another?"[12] Further, (as noted) if long hair is substituted for a cloth covering in verses 5 and 6, the passages make no sense whatsoever (e.g., "If your hair is cut short, then let it be cut short"). If Paul's main concern in chapter 11 is to teach women that they must come to the worship service with long hair then why not simply teach on the necessity of women having long hair all the time as a law of nature. There would be no reason to have a separate discussion about long hair in public worship because a woman's hair is not something that can be removed and replaced in a moment when one desires. Also, the idea that the head covering is long hair would require one to interpret the head covering in reference to men in verse 4 as long hair, which is extremely unlikely.

Paul's reference to long hair as a natural covering comes in a series of reasons for the use of a cloth covering in public worship. The argument for long hair takes one of Paul's sub-points for the use of a cloth veil and makes it the main proposition of the whole section. *If Paul's only and main concern was simply that women keep their hair long while men keep their hair short, then why not begin the discussion with this point? Also, why would Paul use a word for a cloth covering throughout his argument and then use a different Greek word in verse 15 if he was only concerned about hair styles?* One of the greatest problems for the long hair argument is that short lesbian-like hair on women and long effeminate styles on men is not simply a problem for public worship but is also a clear violation of God's law relating to maintaining the God ordained difference between the sexes. If women were trying to look like men, which was common lesbian behavior in the Greco-Roman world, Paul would have dealt with this perverse behavior in his section on sexual immorality and would not have treated the matter as something only improper in public worship.

Obviously then, the apostle is pointing to nature or the natural order where a woman's long hair is a natural covering as supporting evidence for the use of a cloth covering in public worship. "The implication is that as nature has provided women with a head-dress of hair, she is intended, not, of course, to consider this as a substitute for further covering, but to wear a head- dress when she is praying to God in the company of men, nature being regarded as supplying the norm even for such attire...

Regarding the argument in favor of long hair as a covering one more thing needs to be noted. It has been the experience of this author that virtually everyone (pastors, elders, sessions, individuals) who argues for long hair as a covering in public worship, does not require women to have long hair. Why is this fact important? It is important because it reveals that at least for many people the long hair argument is little more than an excuse to avoid the real sign of submission-- a cloth head covering."

Paul's mention of Angels refutes the custom argument because Angels cover themselves in worship.

Isa 6: 2 Seraphim stood above Him, each having six wings: with two he covered his face, and with two he covered his feet, and with two he flew.

Paul's mention of Nature refutes the custom argument. Schwertley says,

"First, it presupposes that Paul was enforcing a Greek custom with no historical or textual support. Was it the universal practice of Greek or Roman women to walk about in public veiled as the cultural argument assumes? If it can be established that it was not the common practice for Greek or Roman women to wear veils in public or in their religious rituals, the whole cultural argument falls to the ground. After an exhaustive study of the dominant practice regarding head coverings in Paul's day, the German scholar Oepke essentially concludes that Paul was imposing a biblical custom upon the Greeks that was contrary to their normal practice. Note the following conclusions of his study. He writes:

It used to be asserted by theologians that Paul was simply endorsing the unwritten law of Hellenic and Hellenistic feeling for what was proper. But this view is untenable. To be sure, the veil was not unknown in Greece. It was worn partly as adornment and partly on such special occasions as match-making and marriage (--559), mourning (--559, cf. also Penelope), and the worship of chthonic deities (in form of a garment drawn over the head). But it is quite wrong that Greek women were under some kind of compulsion to wear a veil in public. Plut. may seem to suggest this. ...But the first passage refers to the Roman custom, concerning which Plut. may not have been too well informed, and the second reflects special Laconic customs. Passages to the contrary are so numerous and unequivocal that they cannot be offset by two sayings of the sage of Chaironeia which are not apodictic and which may have been occasioned by special trend. The mysteries inscription of Andania (Ditt. Syll., 736), which gives an exact description of women taking part in the precession, makes no mention of the veil. Indeed, the cultic order of Lycosura seems to forbid it. Empresses and goddesses, even those who maintain their dignity, like Hera and Demeter, are portrayed without veils, whereas hetaerae occasionally wear hoods. Helen appears before Paris with the upper part of the body uncovered, but with a veil. At the time of Tertullian Jewesses were prominent on the streets of North Africa because they wore veils (De Corona, 4, ed. F. Oehler, I [1853], 424 ff.; De Oratione, 22 [CSEL, 20, 193]). Hence veiling was not a general custom; it was Jewish. If the veiling of Jewish women was common in the West, we may presume that it was an accepted rule in the East. The Jew regarded it as typical of Gentile women that they should go about unveiled (Nu. r., 9 on 5:18, Str.-B., III, 429).... Yet, though the custom [i.e., of wearing a veil] was applied with particular stringency by the Jews, it was oriental rather than distinctively Jewish. The home city of Paul, i.e., Tarsus, is the frontier. Evidence of the veil in Tarsus is provided by Dio Chrys. Or., 33, 46 and coins bearing the image of Tyche of Tarsus. There are exceptions. But

Tarsus is stricter than the rest of Asia Minor. In general one may say that etiquette as regards the veil becomes stricter the more one moves east. This rule is brought out clearly by the provisions of an old Assyrian code. Married women and widows must be veiled when in public places. On the other hand, the head of the harlot, here equated with the slave, must remain unveiled under threat of severe penalties. When a man wishes to make one of these his legitimate wife, a special act of veiling is demanded. Paul is thus attempting to introduce into congregations on Greek soil a custom which corresponds to oriental and especially Jewish sensibility rather than Greek. In principle the demand ought to extend to all women in all situations. In practice, however, Paul applies it to married women in the churches, and in the first instance he restricts it to the sphere of life which stands directly under the jurisdiction of the congregation, i.e., divine worship."[Oepke, "Kalupto" in Gerhard Kittle, ed., Theological Dictionary of the New Testament (Grand Rapids: Eerdmans, 1965), 3:562-563. Emphasis added.]

McKnight notes that William Ramsay, who was an expert on the

Greek culture of Paul's day, concurs. He writes:

Historically, it was a covering commonly worn in public by women of Jewish origin but not by the Greek women. The covering used by Jewish women is thought by many commentators to have been a large piece of cloth which was a common article of clothing such a shawl or cape. The cloth would serve as a head covering at any time it was appropriate. Concerning the difference in Greek and Jewish custom, we find that Dion Chrysostom (writing in 110 A. D.) recognized nothing that was "Greek" about the Tarsians (of the Greek city of Paul); but he did find one thing worthy of praise. He was very pleased with the extremely modest dress of the Tarsian women, who were always deeply veiled when they went abroad. And this was in spite of the fact that it was utterly different from the Greek customs. (The Cities of St. Paul, William Ramsay, p. 202). In other words, a covering was not the custom in other cities and especially Greek cities."[Clyde McKnight, Concerning The Head Covering, Internet article, http:/home:texoma.net/~moses/headc over.htm.]

If it was the cultural practice of Greek or Roman women to wear head coverings in public or during their religious rituals, then one could understand the argument from culture. But, the teaching of Paul was in direct contrast to the Greco-Roman practices of that day.[There was a cult in the Greco-Roman world where both men and women covered their heads during the pagan sacrifice. This practice, however, was not something that influenced the apostle's teaching on public worship at all. Jewish men began to cover their heads in the public service of the synagogues probably a few generations after the close of the N.T. canon of Scripture. The priests who ministered in the temple service covered their heads during their ministrations. This practice, however, should not be considered a contradiction to Paul's teaching in 1 Corinthians 11 because: (a) the priest sacrificial duty's were ceremonial; (b) the priests were not worshipping in a public service with their families but were serving God by themselves as a special class set apart; (c) The turban on the head of a priest has a completely different meaning them the veil on the head of a woman. (d) The priests were wearing a special uniform. "Essentially a uniform draws attention to the office or function of person, as opposed to his individual personality. It emphasizes his job rather than his name" (G. J. Wenham, The Book of Leviticus [Grand Rapids: Eerdmans, 1979], 138). Regarding the high priest's dress, Wenham adds: "In putting on these clothes he took to himself all the honor and glory of the high priesthood.... His glorious clothing symbolized the significance of his office. Probably symbolic significance was also attracted to the individual items in the priestly attire, but that now escapes us" (Ibid, 139). Kellogg writes: "The official robes of the high priest marked him...as the servant of the God of the tabernacle, whose livery he wore. For these colours, various modifications of light, all thus had a symbolic reference to the God of light, who made the universe of which the Mosaic tabernacle was a type" (S. H. Kellogg, The Book of Leviticus (Minneapolis, MN: Klock and Klock, 1978 [1899]), 193).] The apostle was not honoring Greek practice, nor was he instructing women to wear cloth veils in worship because their non-use would have been offensive to Greek society. Paul's inspired teaching (if any thing) would have been offensive to Greek culture. It would have been considered a distinctly Jewish or eastern practice. Clearly, the apostle was imposing a biblical practice upon a distinctly pagan culture. The idea that Paul was following Greek culture rather than directing it has no merit whatsoever. What all of this means, then, is that modern American, European, African or Asian culture must submit to Paul's directives in 1 Corinthians 11 whether or not his instructions are culturally acceptable or not. The Bible is to direct culture and not the other way around. Further, it has been the experience of this author that modern women throughout the United States do indeed understand the significance and meaning of the head covering. This understanding is one of the reasons that the head covering is so strongly hated and opposed by Feminists of all types.

Second, Paul's example of men with long hair as being against nature would not have been acceptable to many Greeks. James Moffat writes:

[H]is Greek hearers must have welcomed an appeal to nature. But they would be taken aback by being asked if long hair was not disgraceful for men. What of the long-haired Spartan heroes in far-off days? What of philosophers at the present day who wore their hair long as an ascetic trait, or to show their indifference to the world? Why, 'the Greek wears long hair on his head because he is a Greek, not a barbarian,' as the moralist Apollonius protested (Epist. viii.). Paul thought it effeminate, however, and praised the braided tresses (I Pet. iii. 3) of women as not merely a glory, or ornament, but as a sort of covering.

The implication is that as nature has provided woman with a head-dress of hair, she is intended, not, of course, to consider this as a substitute for further covering, but to wear a head-dress when she is praying to God in the company of men, nature being regarded as supplying the norm even for such attire.[James Moffatt, The First Epistle of Paul to the Corinthians (London: Houghter and Stoughton, 1958), 154.]

When considering ancient hair styles Aune writes:

Long hair was often regarded by the Greeks a sign of effeminacy in male (H. Herter, "Effeminatus," RAC 4:629) or moral laxity in a female Ps. Phocylides 212). Fashions change, however, for Greek men once favored long hair (Herodotus 1. 82; Plutarch Lysander 1; co. Plato Phaedo 89 B-C) though by the fifth century B. C., only

Spartan men wore their hair long (Aristophanes Aves 1281-82; Philostratus Vita Apoll. 8.7). The Romans wore their hair long until the third century B. C., after which they considered long hair either barbaric or old fashioned (Juvenal 5.30). The Gauls wore their hair long, and as a result northern Gaul was called Gallia Comata, "long-haired Gaul." Apollonius of Tyana, following the practice of philosophers, wore his hair disheveled (Philostratus Vita Apoll. 8.7). Parthian warriors wore their hair long (Plutarch Crassus 24.2), and many interpreters have understood the demonic locust army as mytho-poetic imagery for the Parthian threat (see Excursus 16A: Rome and Parthia). [David E. Aune, Revelation 6-16 (Nashville: Thomas Nelson, 1998), 532]

The teaching of Paul that long hair on a man is shameful was not universally accepted in the ancient world, nor is it accepted today."

This appeal to nature is made numerous times in scripture to speak to sexual issues.

Deut. 22: 5 "A woman shall not wear man's clothing, nor shall a man put on a woman's clothing; for whoever does these things is an abomination to the Lord your God.

Rom. 1: 26 For this reason God gave them over to degrading passions; for their women exchanged the natural function for that which is unnatural, 27 and in the same way also the men abandoned the natural function of the woman and burned in their desire toward one another, men with men committing indecent acts and receiving in their own persons the due penalty of their error.

In Gal 3:28 Paul was simply stating that race or gender does not bar one from entering the Covenant of Abraham, via Messiah. If this verse is doing away with gender distinctions it follows very clearly then that women can become Elders and marry each other. This is why liberal denominations have flourished so well in our post racial society: by taking these anti-racial and egalitarian interpretations of Paul and the Law. Those who believe in the liberation of women must allow women to be preachers and to allow sodomites to marry. That is the consistent logical implication of this philosophy. Also this passage would only speak to those who are in Messiah. What of those outside of him? Do they get de-racialized and de-sexed because of Messiah too? Do we have the Eastern Orthodox Christus Victor Universal atonement raising its head here? Thus, the context here is not secular, sexual and racial. It is ecclesiastical. Yeshua dissolves the significance of race as it regards covenant status. He does not dissolve race itself. Thus the Christian anti-racist position conflates substance with mode and circumstance.

Objections

When faced with these devastating facts modern women will unusually throw up two objections:

1. What about the education of women?

Ans. This is a continuum fallacy. In keeping with Protestant tradition, all peoples in our country should be taught basic skills such as reading, math, history, etc. that they may read the scriptures and feed from them. However, that a woman should put herself in debt to attend college, and drive herself to compete with men in the world, thus eliminating her ability to raise a family, is a clear violation of Scripture.

*Titus 2: 3 Older women likewise are to be reverent in their behavior, not malicious gossips nor enslaved to much wine, teaching what is good, 4 so that they may encourage the young women to love their husbands, to love their children, 5 to be sensible, pure, **workers at home**, kind, being subject to their own husbands, so that the word of God will not be dishonored.*

2. Abortions take place whether they are legal or illegal!

Ans. This is another continuum fallacy. During prohibition alcohol was illegal but people still got drunk. That doesn't mean that prohibition did not keep a lot of people from drinking. Far less people got drunk during prohibition than after.

In conclusion, I would plead with any female reader that considers herself liberated to reconsider her dishonest, insulting, shameful, disgraceful, ungrateful, illogical, baseless, ignorant, and quite frankly bloodthirsty attitude toward men, toward children and toward her responsibilities in society. May Yah grant our nation repentance before Rome grabs complete control of this dis-unified, demoralized and ignorant apostate Protestant Nation and we find ourselves right back under the Inquisition that our Fathers fled from 400 years ago.

End

www.ingramcontent.com/pod-product-compliance
Lightning Source LLC
Chambersburg PA
CBHW022129170526
45157CB00004B/1807